SCHIRMER'S LIBR

OF MUSICAL CLASSICS

Vol. 2130

SELECTED PIANO MASTERPIECES

UPPER INTERMEDIATE LEVEL

28 Pieces by 12 Composers

ISBN 978-1-4950-8802-5

G. SCHIRMER, *Inc.*

www.schirmer.com
www.halleonard.com

CONTENTS

Prelude
in G minor

Johann Sebastian Bach
BWV 930

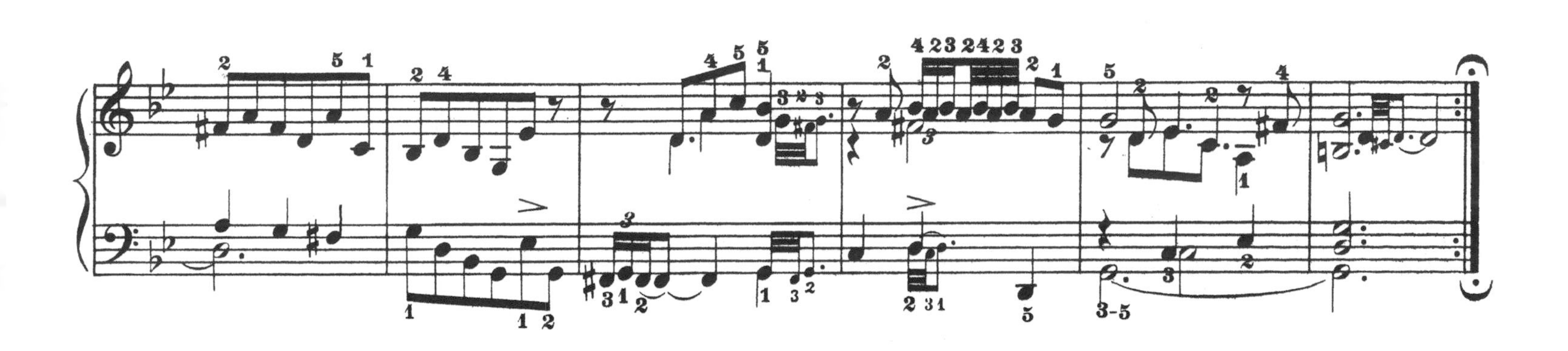

Prelude

in D minor

Johann Sebastian Bach

BWV 935

Bear Dance

from *Ten Easy Pieces*

Béla Bartók

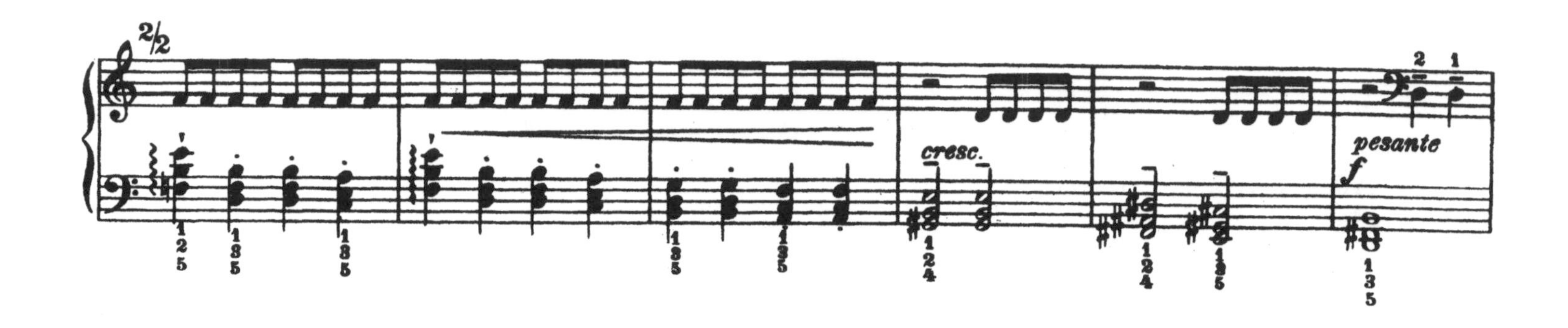
cresc.
pesante

poco allarg.
a tempo
molto marcato
sim.

sim.

dim.

cresc.
f pesante
poco allarg.
a tempo
poco marcato
sempre p
dim.

à Monsieur le Comte de Perthuis

con anima
1.
2.
cresc.
p
a tempo
riten.
dim.
sempre più p
riten.
pp

Mazurka

in A minor

Frédéric Chopin
Op. 67, No. 4
(Posthumous)

rit.
a tempo
cresc.
f
p
mf
marcato
riten.
a tempo
cresc.
dim.
legatissimo

Nocturne

in C minor

Frédéric Chopin
KK. IVb, No. 8

animato
8va

poco più forte
p
mf
p
rit.
a tempo
mf
f
p
8va
rall.
molto cresc.
f

à J. C. Kessler

Prélude

in E Major

Frédéric Chopin
Op. 28, No. 9

à J. C. Kessler

Prélude

in D-flat Major
"Raindrop"

Frédéric Chopin
Op. 28, No. 15

sotto voce
cresc.
p cresc.
ff
dimin.
p
cresc.
p cresc.
ff

fz dimin.
p
p
cresc.
f
p
p
dim. e rit.
smorzando
e
slentando
f
p
pp
riten.

à J. C. Kessler

Prélude

in C minor

Fréderic Chopin
Op. 28, No. 20

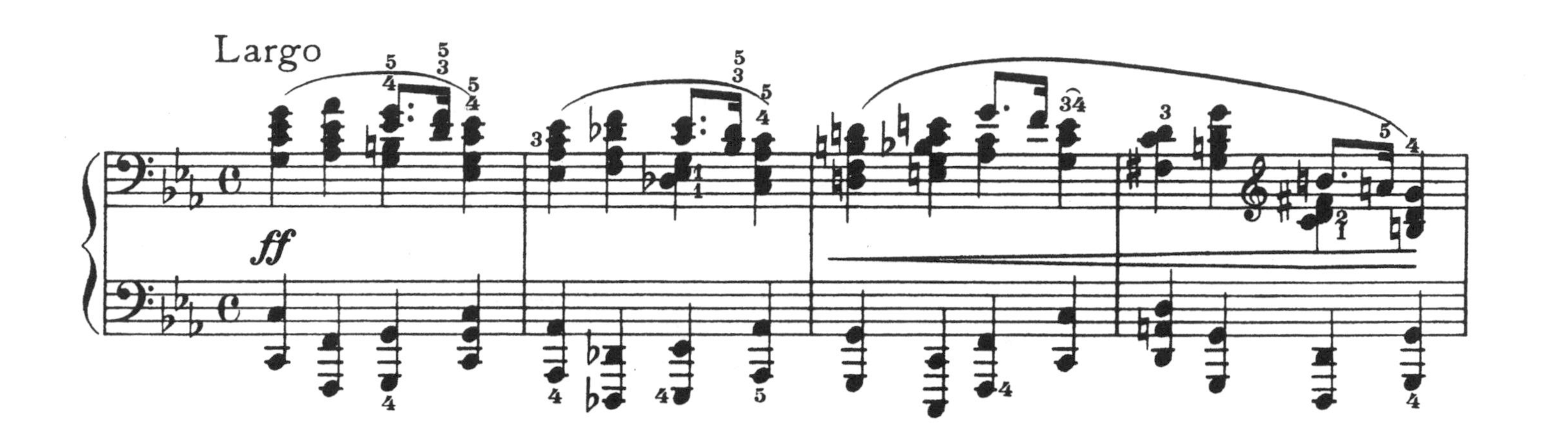

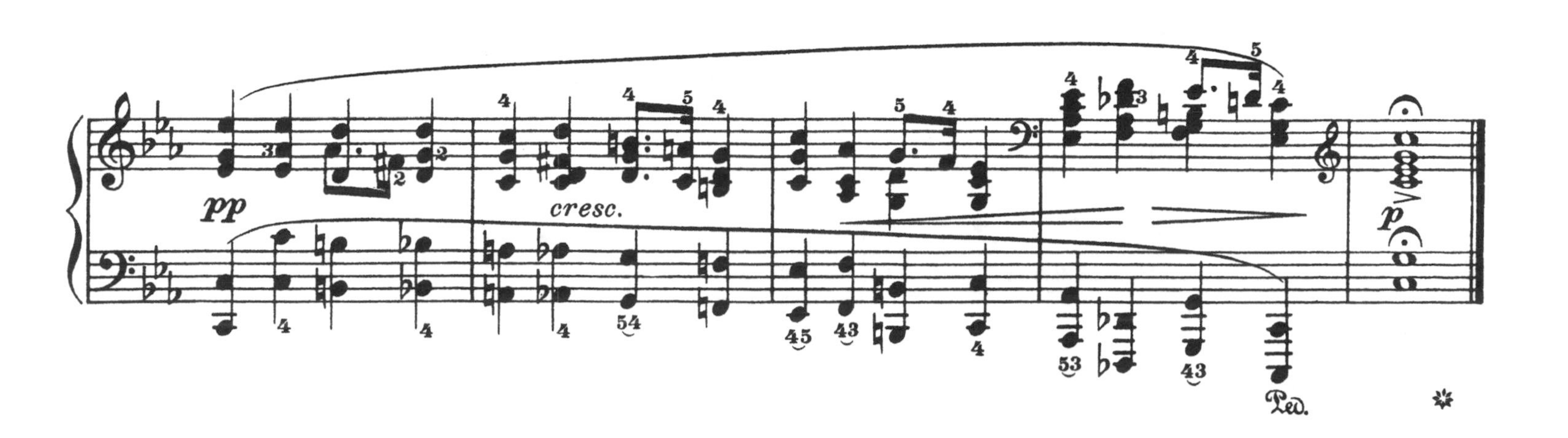

Waltz
in B minor
Frédéric Chopin
Op. 69, No. 2
(Posthumous)
Moderato (♩= 152)
p
sf
p
cresc.
riten.
dim.
a tempo
p
rf
dim.
p
mf
riten.
dim.
a tempo

con anima
rit.
tempo
f
sf
sf
rit.
a tempo
1.
2.
a tempo
mf dolce

cresc. un poco
dim.
mf
cresc.
dim.
sf
p
f
p
rit.
Ped.

dim.
a tempo
con anima
rit.
a tempo
f
sf
sf
rit.
f
calando e dim.

Arabesque No. 1

from *Two Arabesques*

Claude Debussy

p
rit.
a tempo
p
rit.
p
a tempo
p
poco mosso
cresc.
p

Tempo rubato (un peu moins vite) (somewhat slower)
p
sf
mosso
p
cresc.
rit.
mosso
f
p
cresc.
a tempo
f
f
p

risoluto
f
rit.
dim. molto
Tempo I°
più dim.
p
rit.
a tempo
p
poco a poco cresc.
stringendo
sempre cresc.
rit.

a tempo
p
3
3
2/4
4/4
4/4
dim.
più dim.
3
p
pp
3
pp

Doctor Gradus ad Parnassum

from *Children's Corner*

Claude Debussy

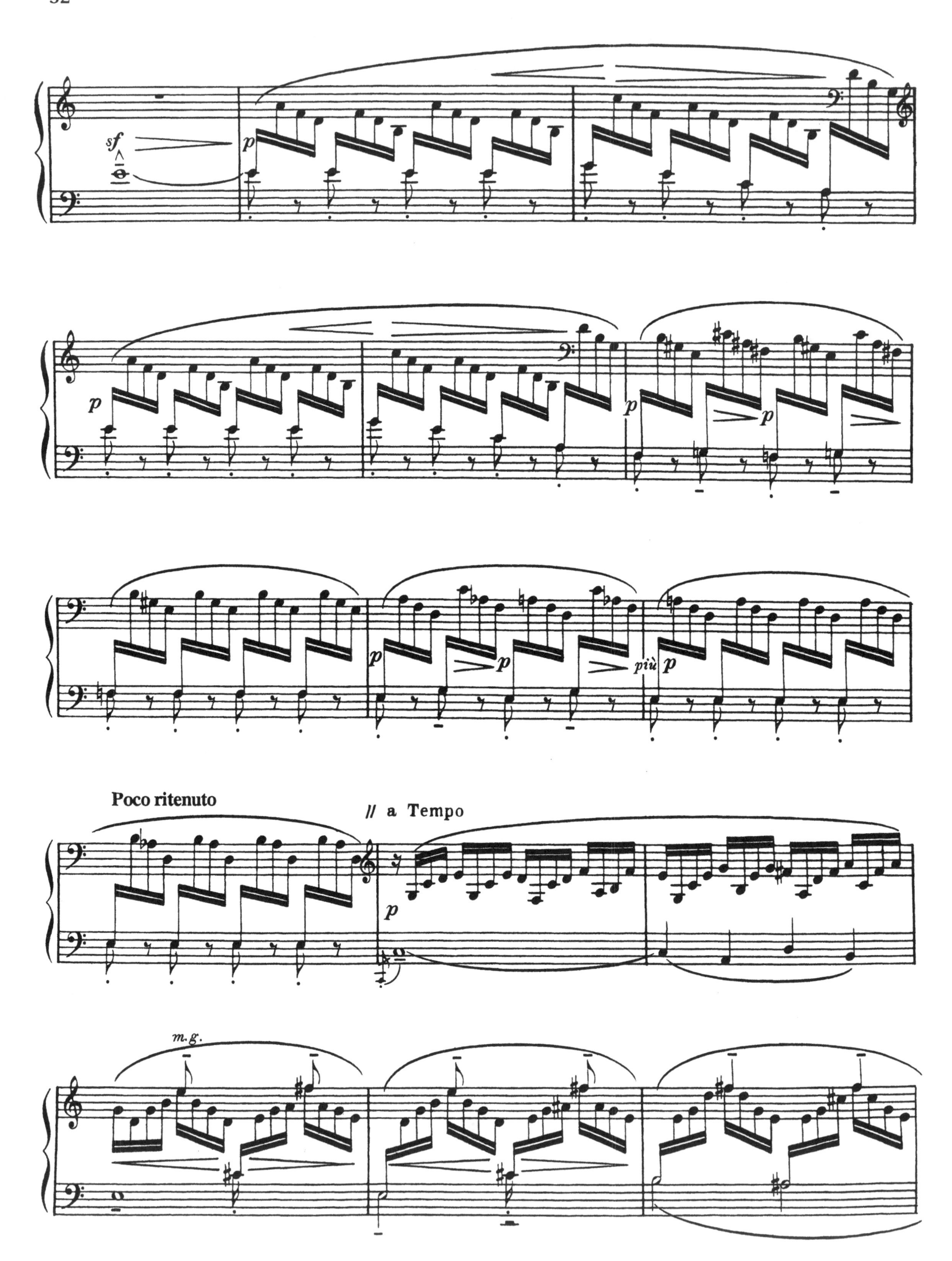
sf
p
p
p
p
p
p
più p
Poco ritenuto
// a Tempo
p
m.g.

m.g.
espressivo
dim.
Ritenuto
Tempo I
p
espressivo
più p
Poco animando
pp
espressivo
espressivo
Ritenuto

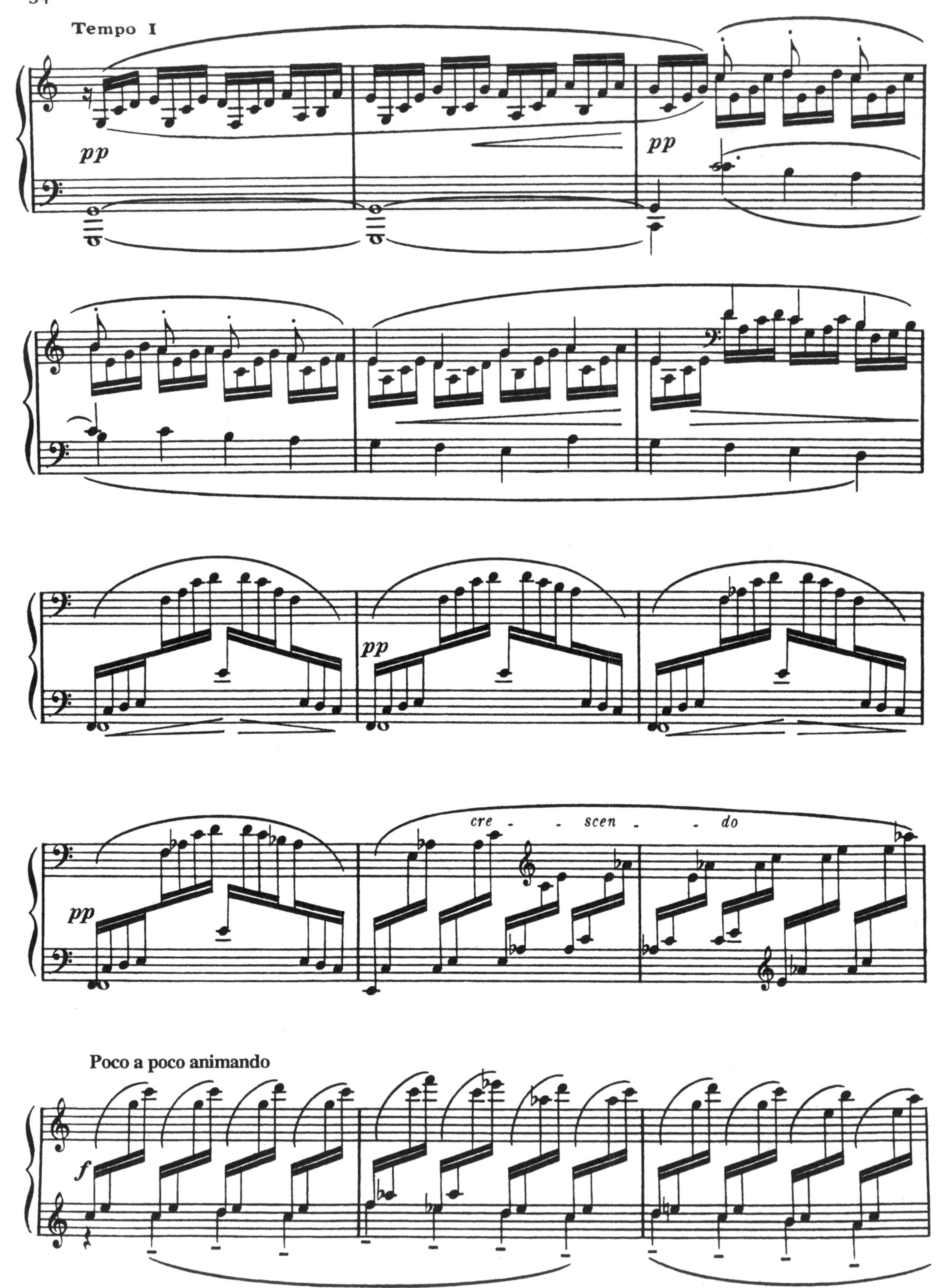

Tempo I
pp
pp
pp
pp
cre - - scen - - do
Poco a poco animando
f

f
Molto animato
f
f
f
f
f
più f
ff
ff
ff

Le petit nègre

Claude Debussy

ritenuto
a Tempo
pp
dolce
ed espressivo
p
pp
p
cresc.
Ritenuto
f

a Tempo
ff
f marcato

mf e dim.
f

mf
dim.

cresc. molto
a Tempo
ff
pp
dolce

ed espressivo
p

pp

p

Ritenuto
cresc.
f

a Tempo

Rêverie

Claude Debussy

pp
3
poco cresc.
più cresc.
f
p
f
p
dim.
pp espress.

pp
sf
mf
dim.
p rit.
p
più p
p
più p

pp
cresc.
mf
p
più p
pp
(l.h.)

l.h.
meno p
p
p
un peu retenu
(a little slower)
p
più p
pp
rit. e perdendosi

March of the Trolls

from *Lyric Pieces*

Edvard Grieg
Op. 54, No. 3

dim. poco a poco
p
dim.
una corda
pp

p cantabile
p
Ped.
Ped.
Ped.
Ped.
pp
Ped.

p
p
Ped.
Ped.
Ped.
Ped.
dim.
Ped.
Ped.
Ped.
Ped.

pp
staccato
sempre pp
una corda
staccato
cresc. poco
tre corde
a poco
molto
ff

dim. poco a poco
p
dim.
una corda
pp
ff

Consolation No. 3

from *Consolations*

Franz Liszt

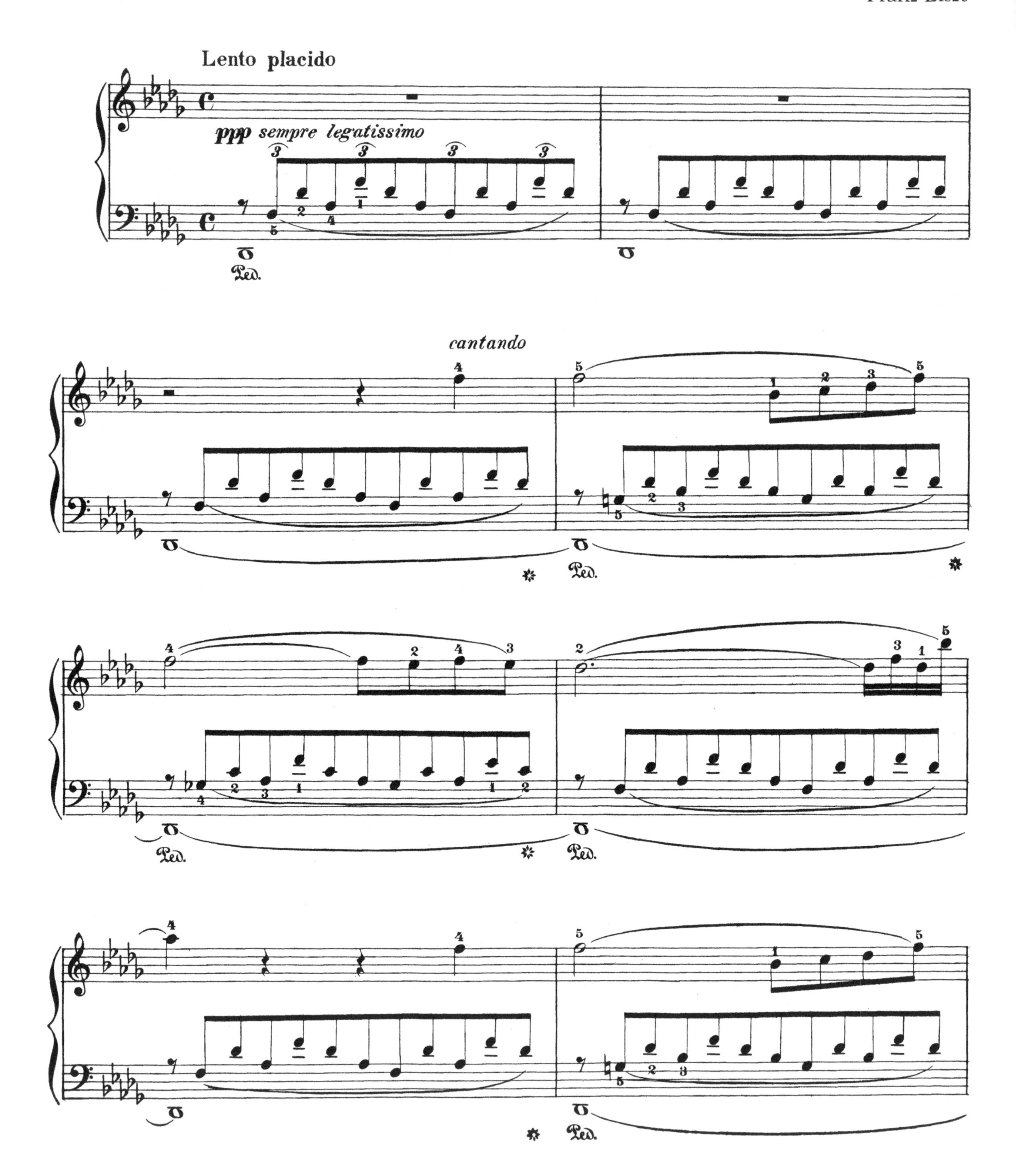

Ped.
mf espressivo

dolcissimo
mf espressivo
dolcissimo

poco rit.

Ped.
Ped.
8
smor - zan - do
ppp
Ped.
8
rit. per - den - dosi

Song Without Words

in F-sharp minor

"Venetian Boat-Song No. 2"

Felix Mendelssohn

Op. 30, No. 6

f
ff
sf
dimin.
Ped.
pp
sf
dimin.
p
p
cresc.
al
f
dim.
p
cresc.
al
f
sf
dim.
sf
p
dim.
pp

Prelude
in E minor
Alexander Scriabin
Op. 11, No. 4
Lento ♩ = 72-80
p
pp
cresc.
mf
p
pp
pp
pp
ppp

à Mademoiselle Jeanne de Bret

Three Gymnopédies*

1

Erik Satie

* Ceremonial choral dance performed at ancient Greek festivals.

p

(1)-3
2
1
4
2
1
pp
ped. simile
3
pp
1
4
f
pp

p

à Conrad Satie

2

pp
f
pp

à Charles Levade

3

pp
p
pp
pp

Moment musical

in A–flat Major

from *Six moments musicaux*

Franz Schubert

Op. 94, No. 2

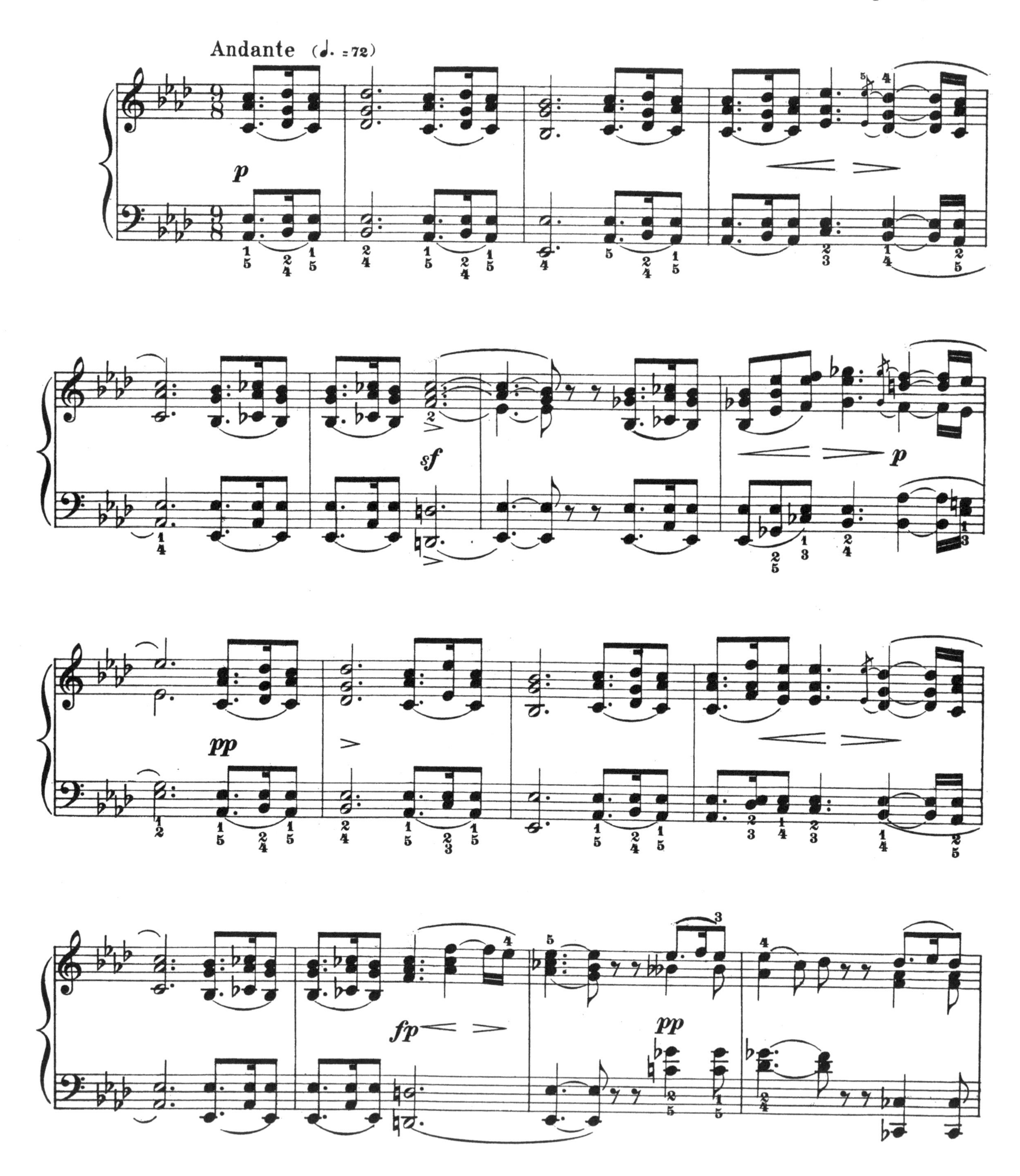

f
p
pp
cresc.
pp
p
p
pp

p
pp
cresc.
pp
f
p

pp
p
pp
pp
pp
f
p
pp

Bittendes Kind

(Pleading Child)

from *Scenes from Childhood*

Robert Schumann

Op. 15, No. 4

Träumerei

(Reverie)

from *Scenes from Childhood*

Robert Schumann
Op. 15, No. 7

Mignon

from *Album for the Young*

Robert Schumann

Op. 68, No. 35

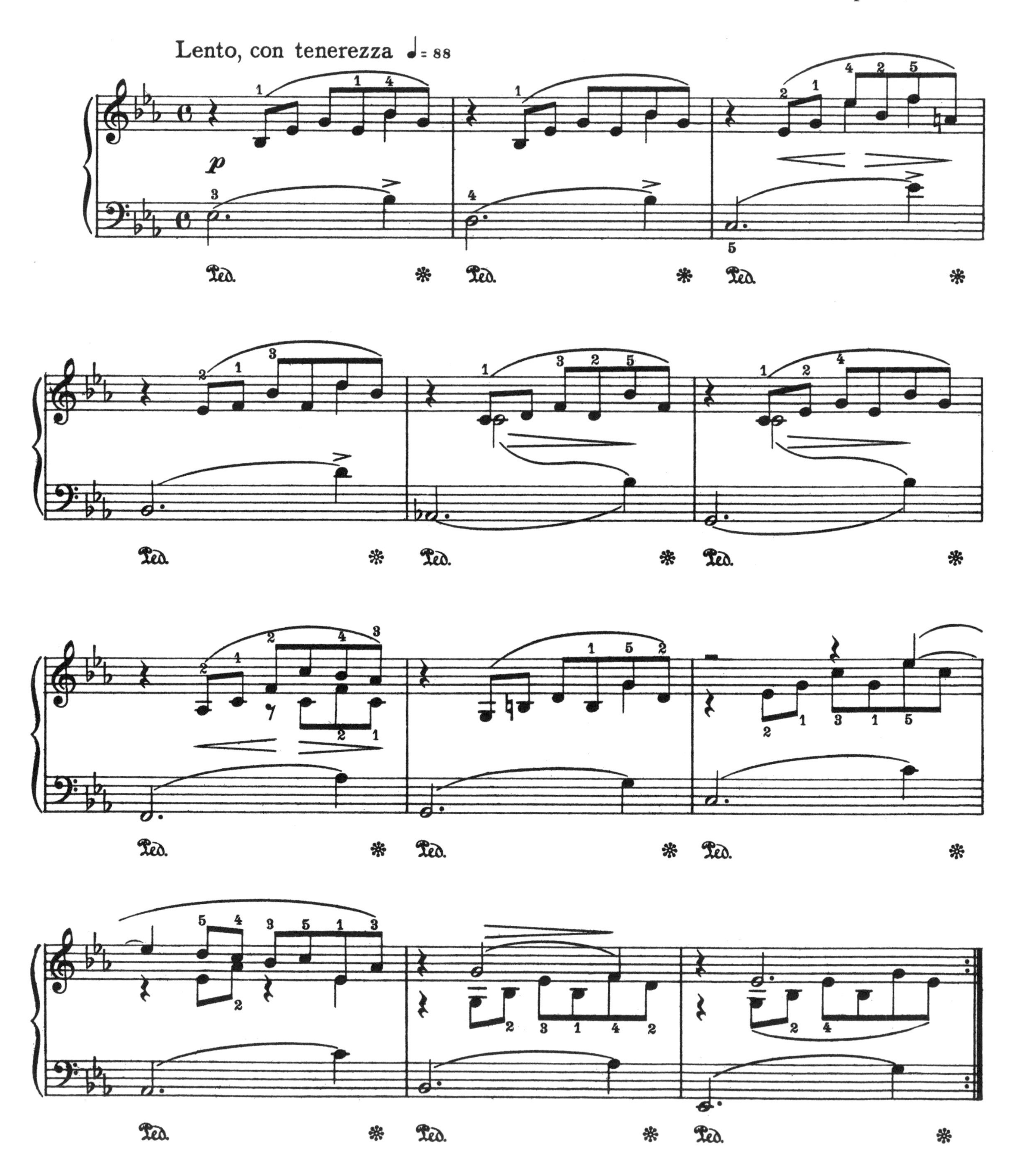

mf
f
Ped.
p
cresc.
pp
dim.
rit.
1.
2.

Chanson triste

from *12 Pieces*

Pyotr Il'yich Tchaikovsky
Op. 40, No. 2

f
p
poco rit.
p a tempo
f
p
mf
p
pp
ppp